The Book Authority Guide on Why You Should Write a Book

John Kremer, The Book Authority

The Authority on Writing Books

The Authority on Publishing Books

The Authority on Marketing Books

John Kremer
P O Box 271
Dolan Springs AZ 86441

575-741-1581

Web: https://www.BookAuthorAuthority.com

Table of Contents

39 Reasons Why You Should Write a Book

The sooner you write a book, the better (for you and your business). Books give you credibility and authority. Books build your expertise and your value. Books enable you to grow your business. As an author, you become qualified to speak, to coach, to consult, even to build and sell other products.

Indeed, you can write a book in ten days or less! You can even write a book in less than five days or seven days. Find out more at https://www.BookAuthorAuthority.com.

On the next 39 pages, I showcase and describe 39 reasons why you should write a book. Pick one or two reasons, and start writing your book.

1. Make money.

You can make money not only by selling your book, but also by selling all the ancillary products and services you can offer.

Money is often the key motivator for many authors, but it certainly isn't the only reason why you should write a book.

2. Change lives.

39 Reasons Why You Should Write a Book

Change Lives

BookAuthorAuthority.com

Books can enlighten, educate, inspire, inform, and entertain. They can and do change lives.

Everyone has at least one story of a book that changed their lives. What book changed your life? Now, write one to change other people's lives.

3. Sell a product.

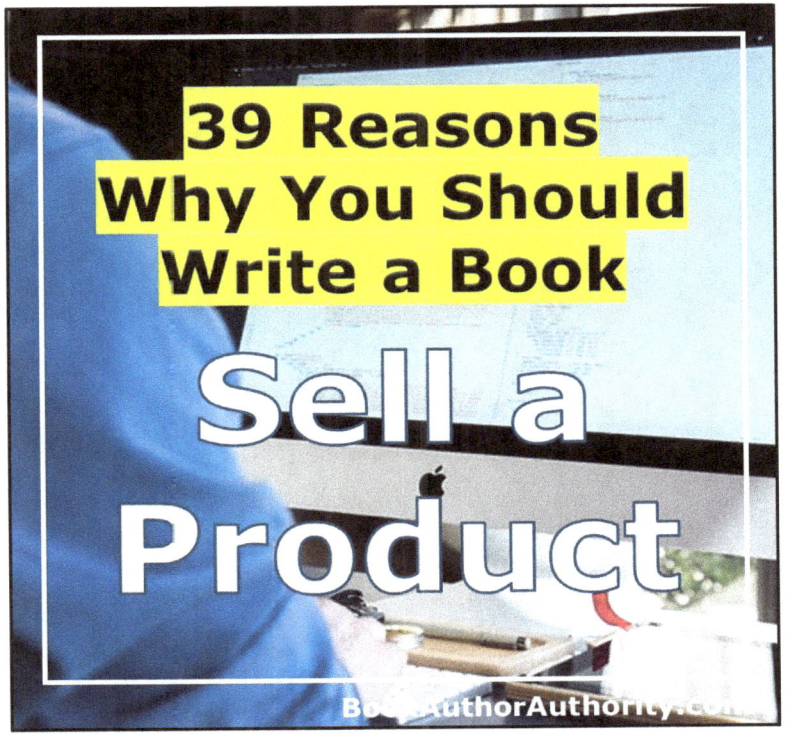

Use your book to help promote another product, whether a real world product or an online information product. Books can help you sell all your other products and services.

Seed your book with the stories of your other products and services. Include case studies, success stories, examples of failure and success.

Books can sell your products and services faster and easier than anything else. Books allow you to showcase what you do, how well you do it, and how your customers benefit from what you offer.

4. Build a career.

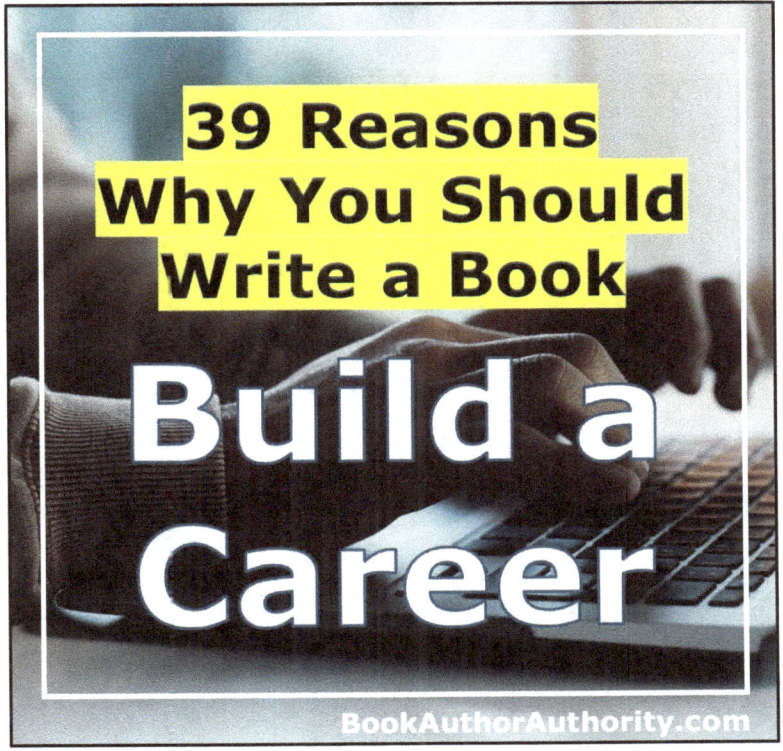

There's no better way to build a career than to start by writing a book. Books open doors. Books get respect. Books get you promotions. And books get you job offers, again and again.

5. Boost your credibility.

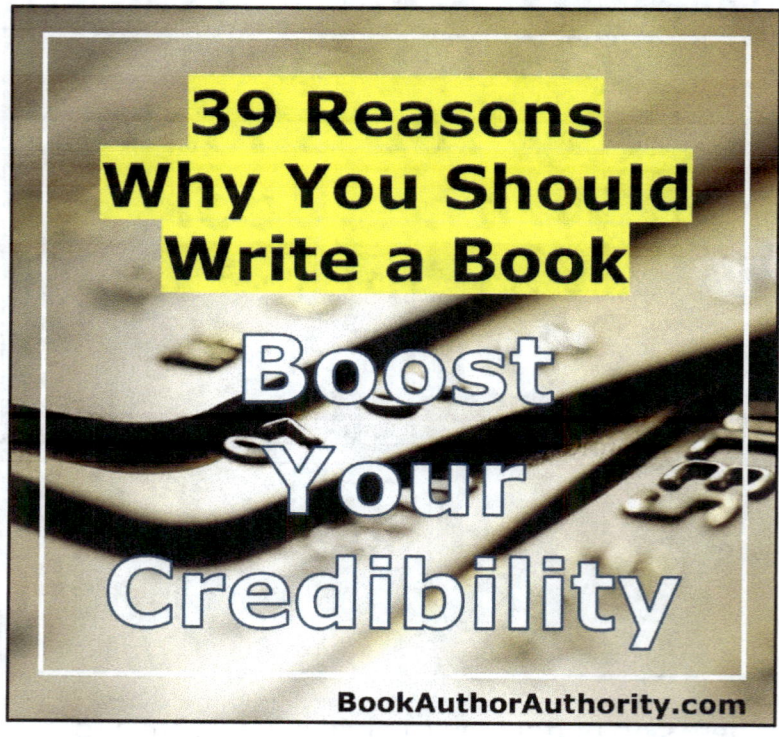

Nothing establishes your authority better than a book. Your book instantly boosts your credibility as a doer, as an expert, as a celebrity, as an authority. Of course, it has to be a good book, a great book, an extraordinary book. The more extraordinary, the more your credibility will grow!

6. Support a cause.

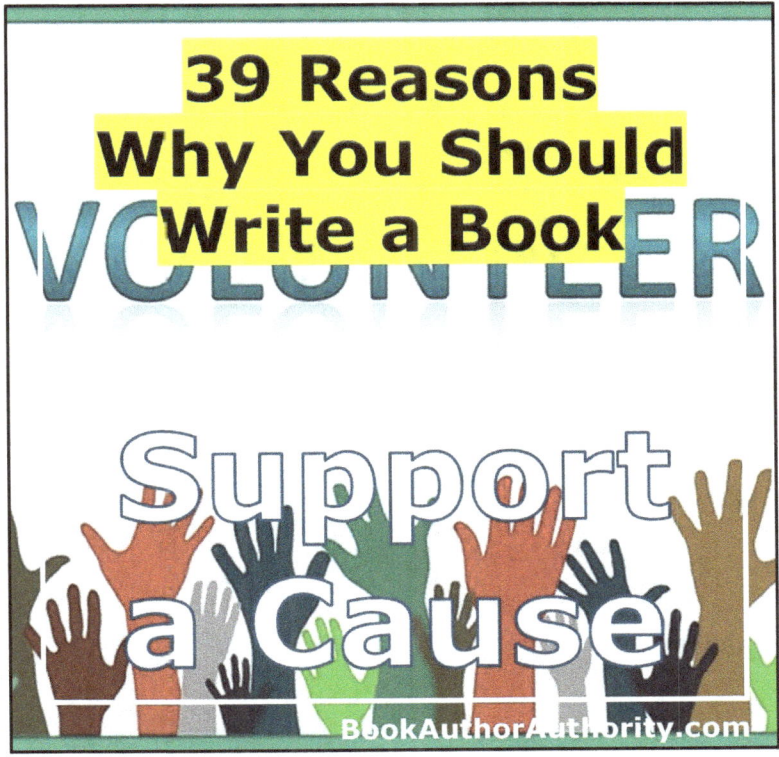

Passionate about the environment? Write a book! Passionate about inner city health? Write a book! Passionate about gun violence? Write a book! Whatever cause you support, you can support it more effectively by writing a book versus donating money or time.

7. Share a message.

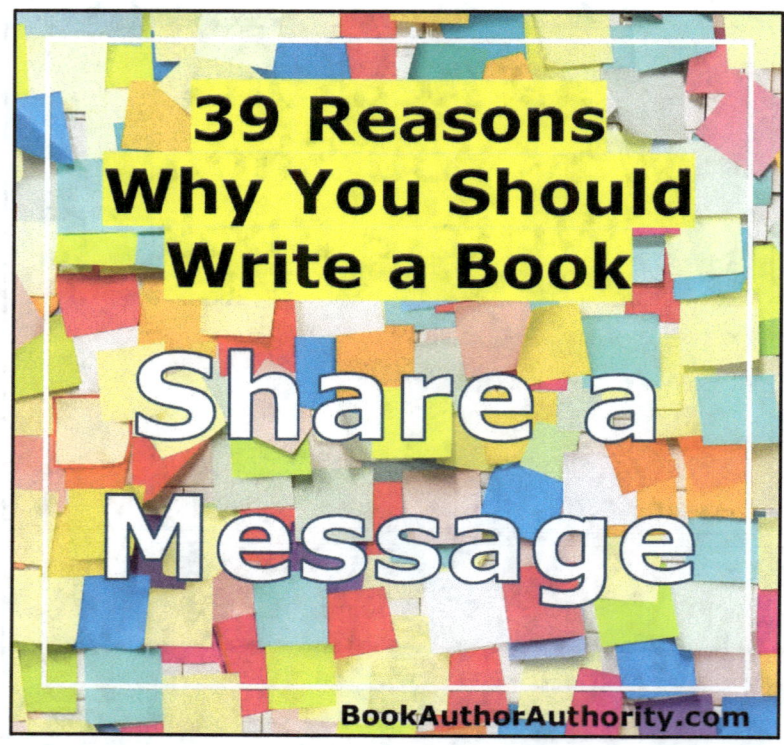

Share a message you've got to get out. We all have magic inside us that wants to get out. Writing a book is one of the best ways to get your magic message out into the world.

8. Build a tribe.

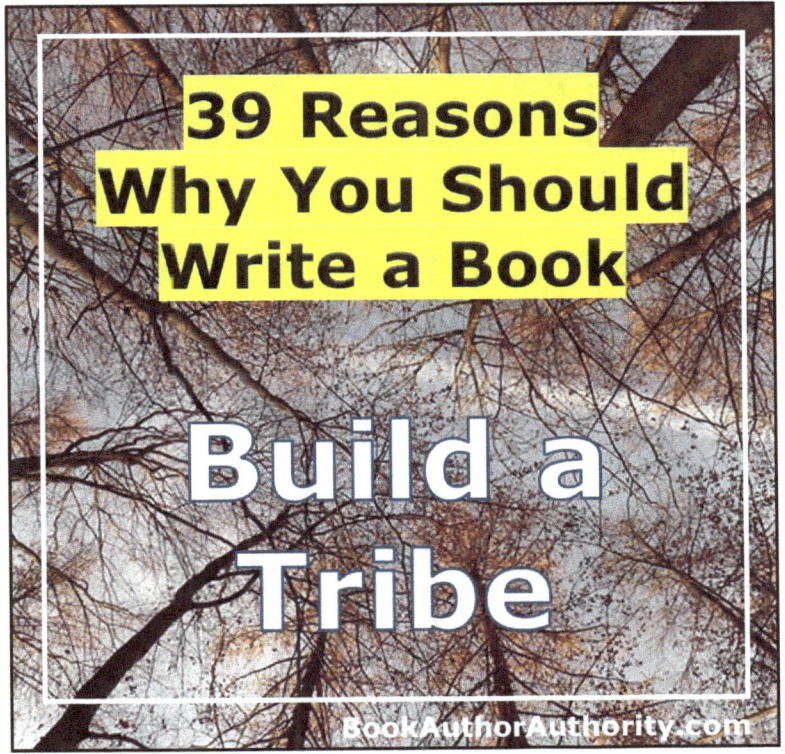

If you want to create a fan club, a following, or a community, write a book! They'll find you! They'll find you not only on the social networks, but also in reading groups, meetups, conferences, and more.

9. Use it as a business card.

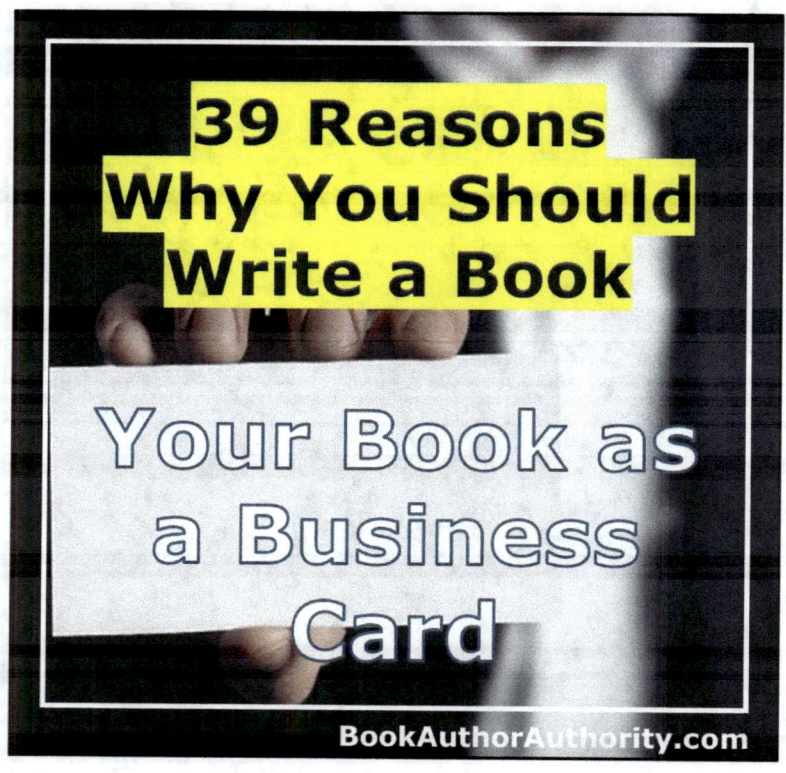

39 Reasons Why You Should Write a Book

Your Book as a Business Card

BookAuthorAuthority.com

Books are the best business card you can carry. Create a very big business card that will get the attention of your customers (and potential customer) and get you more business and sales.

10. Become a speaker.

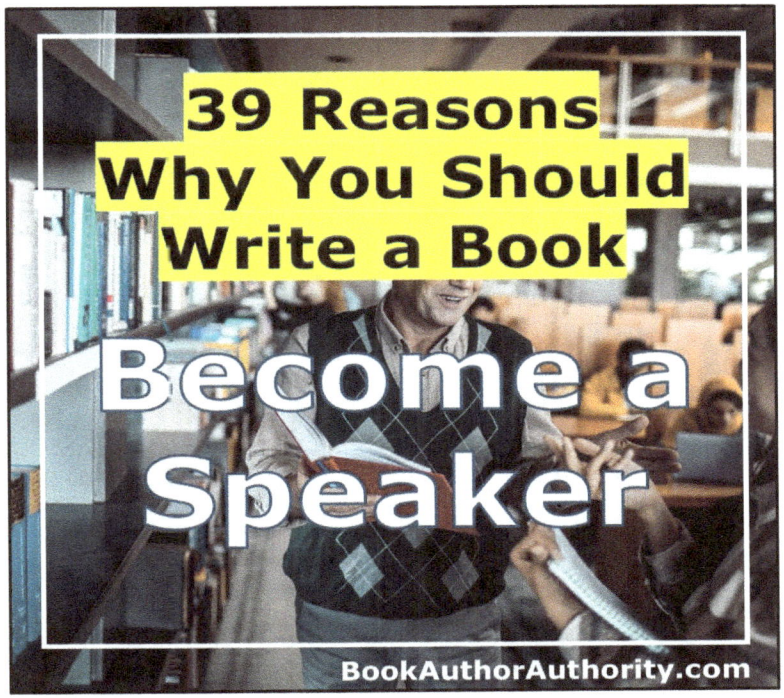

Speakers with a book get more visibility, more bookings, more recognition, and more response. Not only can you speak to outside groups but you can also present and market your own seminars, conferences, webinars, teleconferences, and more.

In addition to your speaking fees (up to $50,000 per speech, but typically between $2,000 and $10,000 per speech), you can build your prospect list fast. Speakers get contact information from 20 to 50% of their audiences.

One speaker reports getting contact information from 97% of his audience, time and time again. That's building an incredible list!

11. Become an expert.

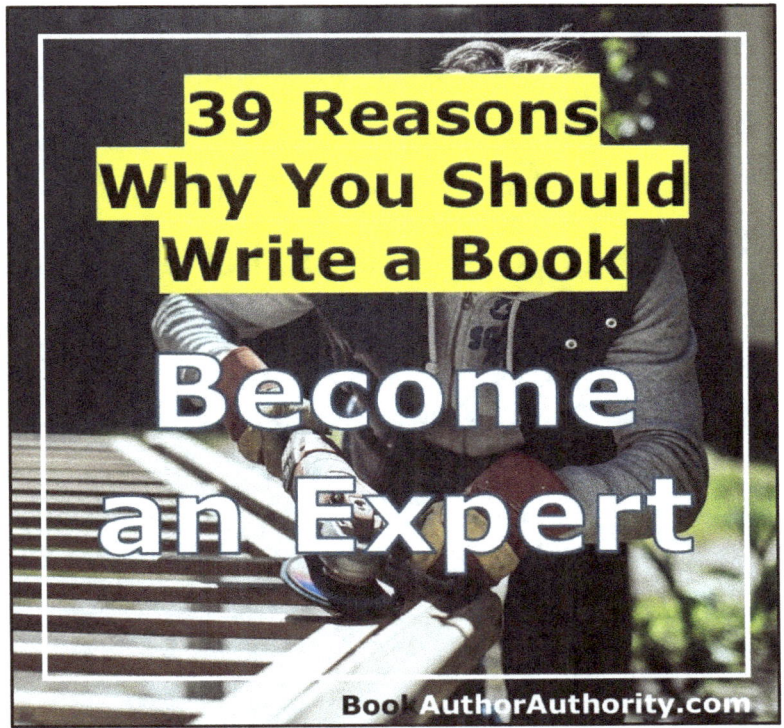

There's no easier way to become an expert in a subject than to write a book about the subject – or THE book on the subject (like *1001 Ways to Market Your Books*). You become an instant expert, a recognizable expert, the minute your book is published.

12. Create new products.

Your book can become the basis for a podcast, audio mp3, Internet radio show, video series, magazine column, syndicated column, webinar series, multimedia course, membership website, etc. Understand that many of your readers actually prefer to absorb information or entertainment in other ways: via audio, via video, via live seminars, via online webinars, via a membership site, via phone calls.

That's why you should always work to take your book and format it for other mediums. It's the quickest and simplest way to create new products.

- ☐ Just take your book, and turn it into an audio.
- ☐ Just take your book, and parcel it out via a membership website.
- ☐ Just take your book, and speak it out live.

13. Be a consultant.

Become a consultant, coach, or mentor. Book authors are the experts people come to when they need answers to their questions. Who would you rather do business with? Someone with a little business card or someone with a bestselling book?

14. Drive traffic to a website.

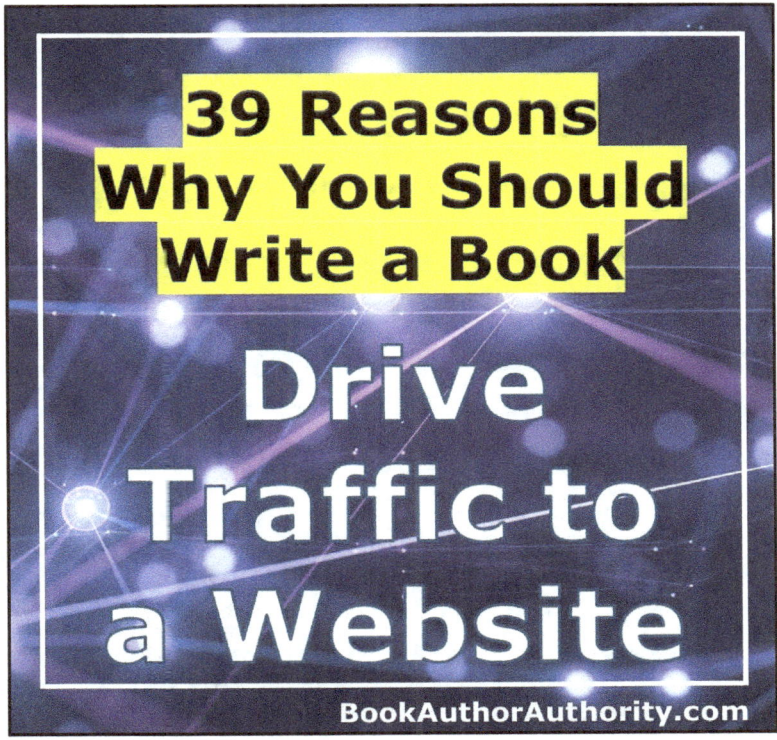

You can use your book to drive readers to different blog articles, online sales pages, email capture pages, podcast episodes, etc. Be sure to include direct response calls to action in all your books!

15. Create and build a business.

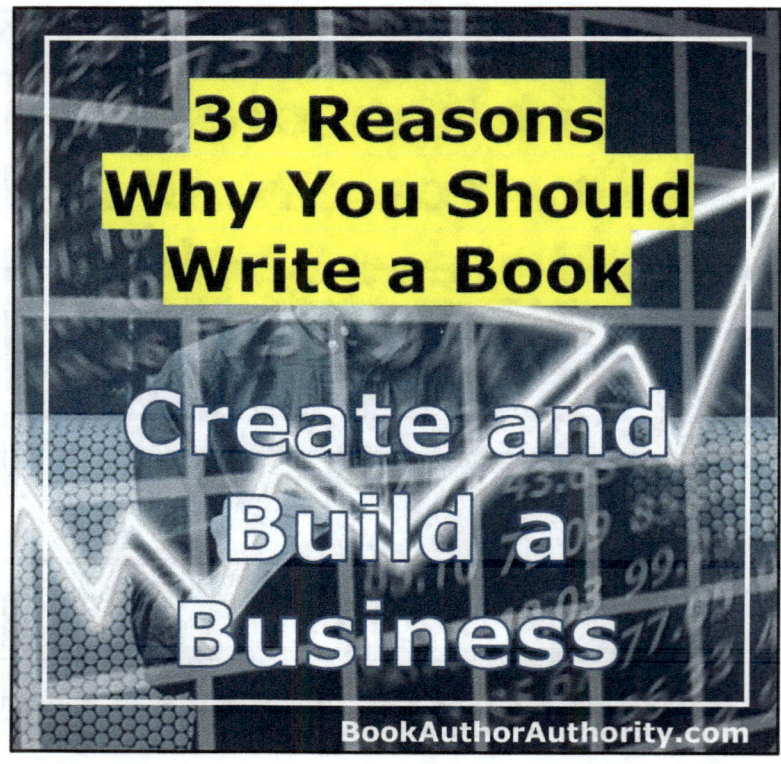

As Mike Koenigs says, you can wrap a business around your book, or you can wrap a book around your business. Your book is your million dollar seed to building a business that will last longer than you do.

16. Become a celebrity.

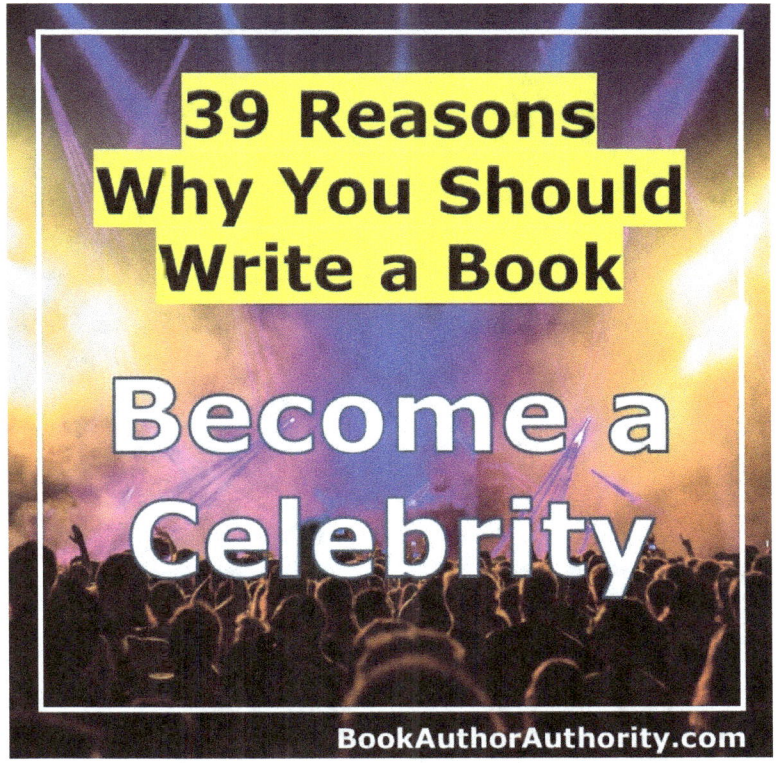

People look up to and idolize book authors. Book authors are celebrities, the kind that can get the best tables in the best restaurants and still leave without getting attacked by the paparazzi.

17. Bypass the gatekeepers!

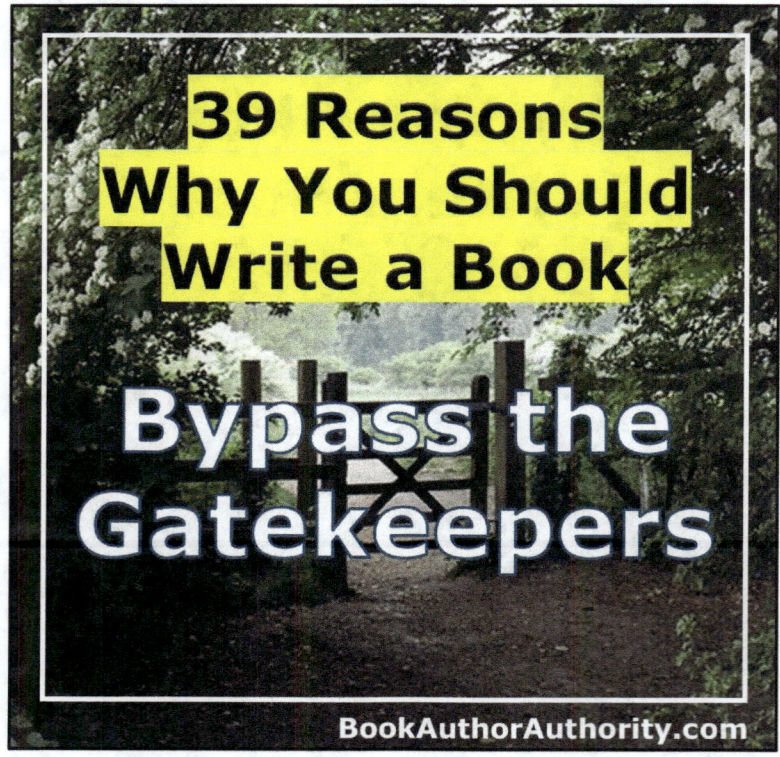

Want to get in the door of major corporations, government offices, foundations, or think tanks? If you are a book author, you can easily get past the gatekeepers to the people you need to talk to. A book is the ultimate foot-in-the-door strategy to get attention from key decision makers.

18. Create wealth.

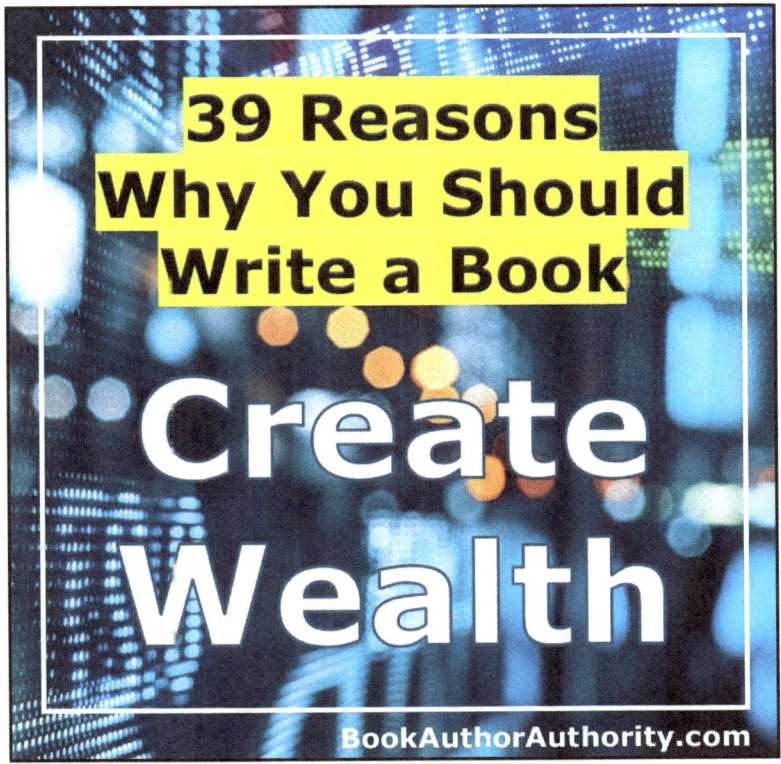

Books can be the foundation to building a great business, a lasting career, or steady income via royalties and rights sales. Many authors report increasing their annual income by $100,000 or more after publishing a book and becoming a bestselling author.

But a note of caution: Many book authors sell fewer than 100 copies of their books. That doesn't create wea th. That's why it's crucial that you learn how to market your books. If you don't take the time to market your books hard, your books won't sell. You won't earn what you are worth. And you won't help people like you want to.

19. Attract better customers.

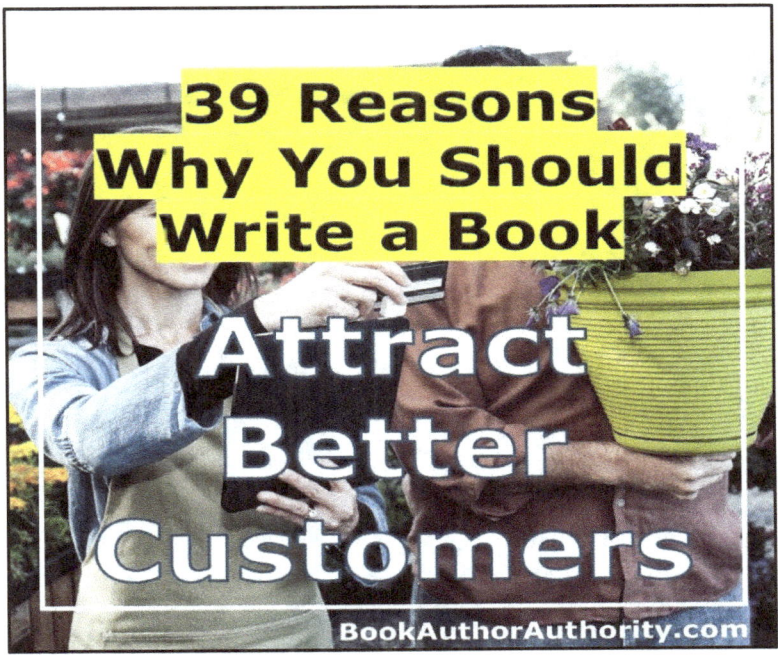

The best way to develop great customers is to give your book to prospective customers. Those prospects who read your book and like it will become your best customers.

Just write a book that answers the top 20 questions that prospects ask you again and again. Prospects always ask better questions after reading a book. If they ask the right questions, they will hire you and keep hiring you. That's the best kind of customer.

20. Market your heavily regulated service.

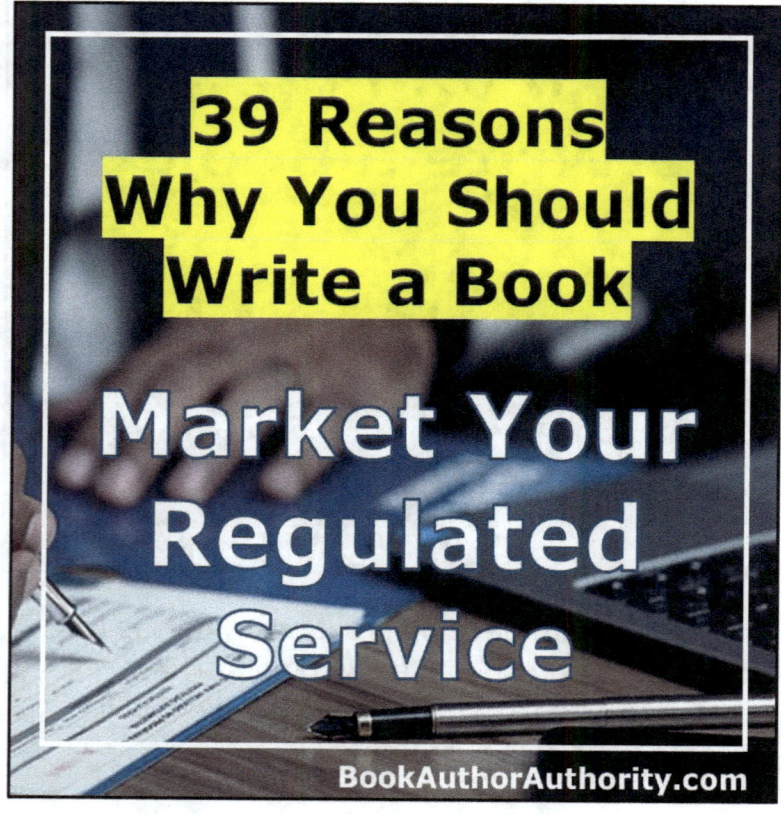

39 Reasons Why You Should Write a Book

Market Your Regulated Service

BookAuthorAuthority.com

If you work in a regulated industry (medicine, drugs, banking, investments, money management, taxes, retirement programs), you can get around the legal teams and compliance departments by writing about your experience.

Compliance can be a stumbling block to marketing your services effectively. But no one can stop you from telling your stories and retelling the stories of your customers.

21. Be free to live the life you want.

Books give you the freedom to live where you want, work when you want, and have more time to cherish your family and friends.

What does success mean to me? It means having choices, legitimate choices, real choices. It means being able to do what I want when I want.

What does success mean to me? It means being able to live where I want — which, for me, means living out in the countryside. I don't like crowds. I hate traffic. I detest city noise. My wife and I live on a graveled country lane where we call it a traffic jam if two cars go by in the same hour. The only noise at night is the sound of crickets and an occasional owl. The air is fresh. The stars are brilliant

What does success mean to me? It means being able to help people, to make it easier for them to live their dreams.

What does success mean to me? It means having enough money to buy the things I need and to take care of my family. I don't need a lot of money. Just enough. I make a comfortable but not extravagant living writing and publishing books. I do just enough to make what I need. The rest of the time I do what I want. I explore new territories. I play. — John Kremer, author and publisher

22. Get maximum publicity.

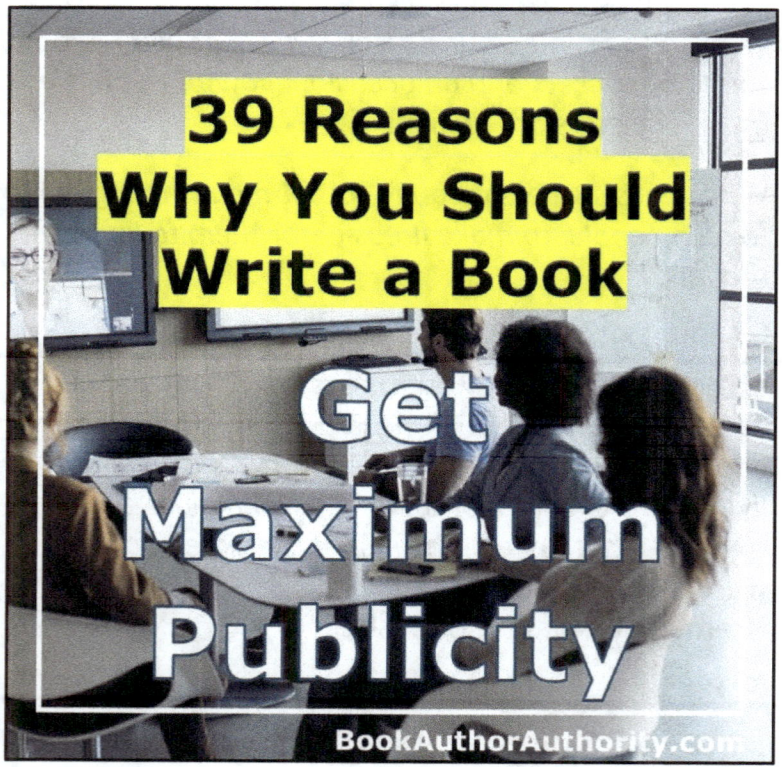

Books are some of the best tools you can use to get publicity, whether local PR or national media attention. Books open doors. Books get attention. Books stand out.

Media are hungry for authors who know what they are talking about and can present their ideas effectively.

Media hosts can use your book to select the topics and questions they want to ask you during an interview. They can also use the search engines (and Amazon) to discover the real experts on any topic. Who are those real experts? Book authors, plain and simple.

23. Become a social media star.

Book authors get more followers on Facebook, Twitter, Pinterest, Instagram, and LinkedIn than do people without a book. Authors are celebrities! They are worth following, friending, fanning, liking, retweeting, and repinning.

Your social media posts can also become the basis for your next book. It's easy to create new books as you continue to post, pin, tweet, and share.

24. Build a local business.

If you don't think a book would help build your local business, ask yourself these four questions (courtesy of Mike Koenig):

- ☐ Do you ever have to fight for business with competitors?
- ☐ Do you have trouble standing out in a crowd?

- ☐ Do you ever get asked the same questions over and over?

- ☐ Do you get price resistance for your services?

If you answer yes to any of the above questions, then writing a book could be the answer to building your local business to a whole new level. A book would help you stand out tall among your competitors. A book would help to answer all the questions prospects ask over and over again. A book would set you apart as the person to work with, even at a premium price!

25. Teach.

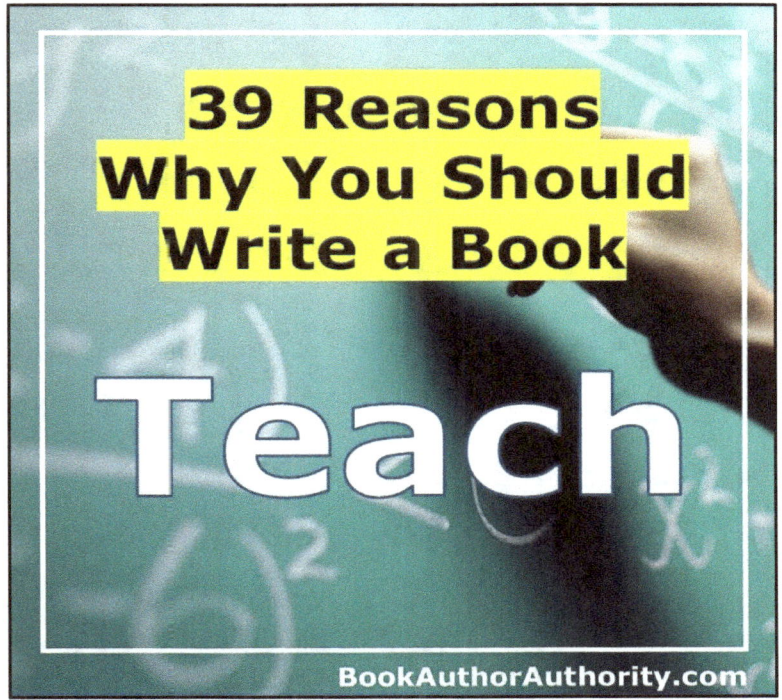

As a book author, you will be offered opportunities to teach in schools and universities, even without a teaching degree, a PhD, or other credential. Your books are your credentials.

26. Serve others.

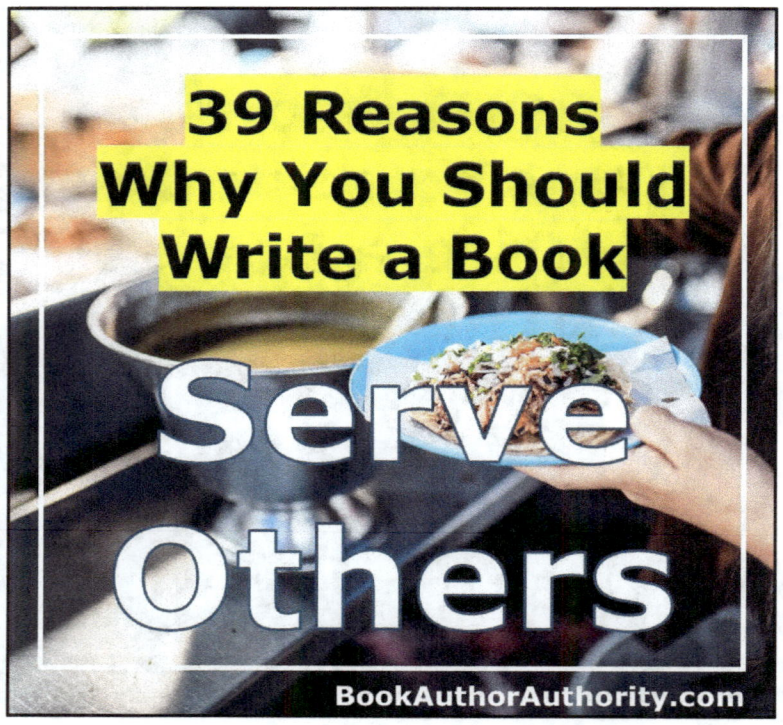

Your books are one of the key ways to serve others by sharing the best of your talent and the best of your ideas.

27. Become a VIP.

39 Reasons Why You Should Write a Book

Become a VIP

BookAuthorAuthority.com

Not only coes writing a book make you an expert and celebrity, but it also guarantees your status as someone who is important, someone who is deserving of respect, someone who people want to be around, someone who draws a crowd wherever you go.

28. Build your list.

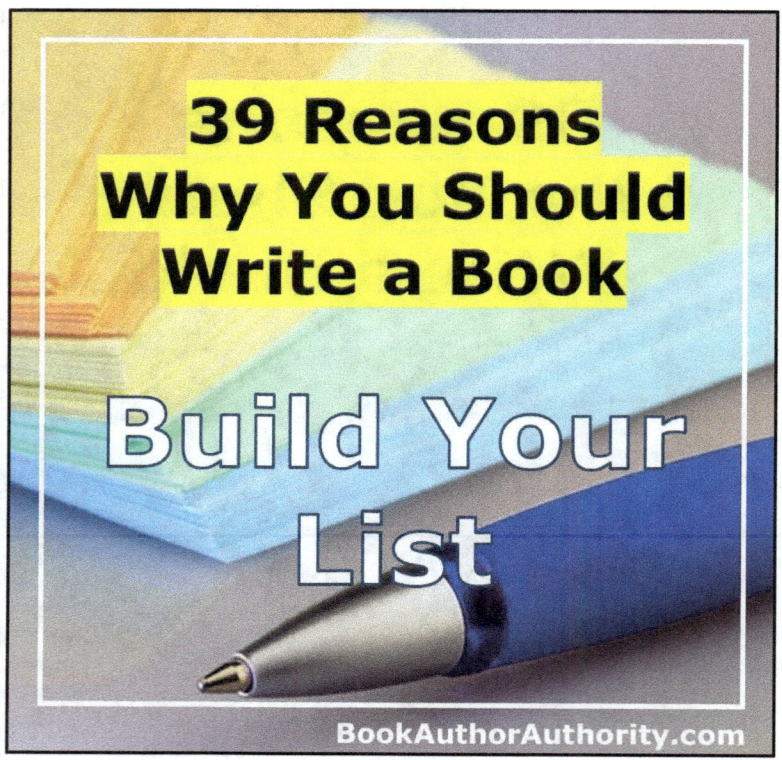

39 Reasons Why You Should Write a Book

Build Your List

BookAuthorAuthority.com

Books are one of the best ways to build a customer list, whether offline or online. By building calls to action within your book, you can send people to a page on your website where you can capture their names and emails.

Every chapter in your book should answer key questions your potential customers have. Each chapter should showcase examples, success stories, and social proof.

If you create great calls to action within your book, you'll generate the same kind of success as other Amazon bestselling authors: For every 10 books they sell on Amazon, they get 2 to 4 leads.

29. Promote live events.

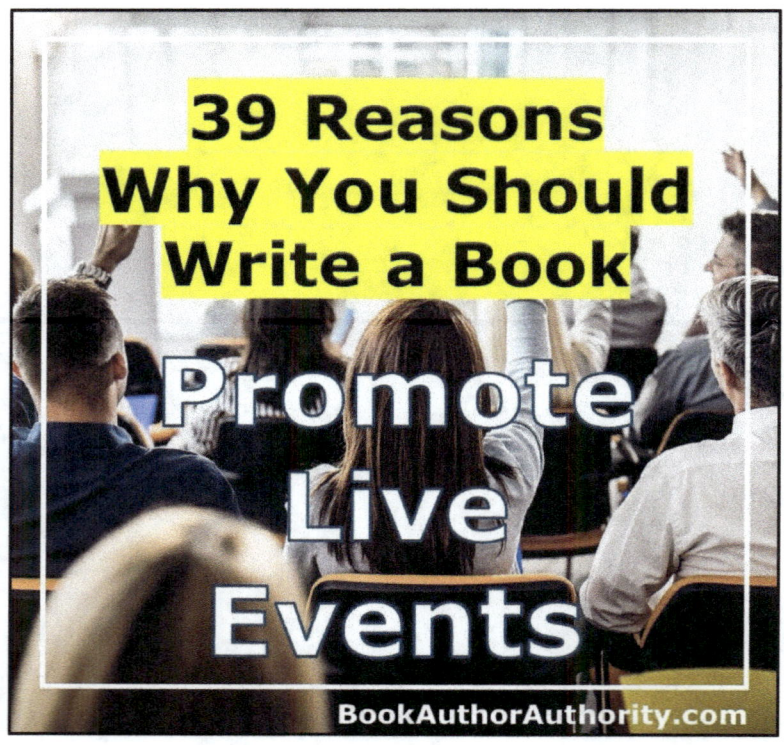

You can use your book to promote your on-going live events: speeches, meetings, seminars, webinars, podcasts, teleseminars, and more.

30. Partner with top companies.

Partner with top companies to sell more books. Work with Apple, Google, YouTube, Amazon, and other high-traffic websites to promote you, your books, your business, your services, and your other products. With a book, you can easily partner with the top websites because they love books and they love book authors.

31. Launch a product.

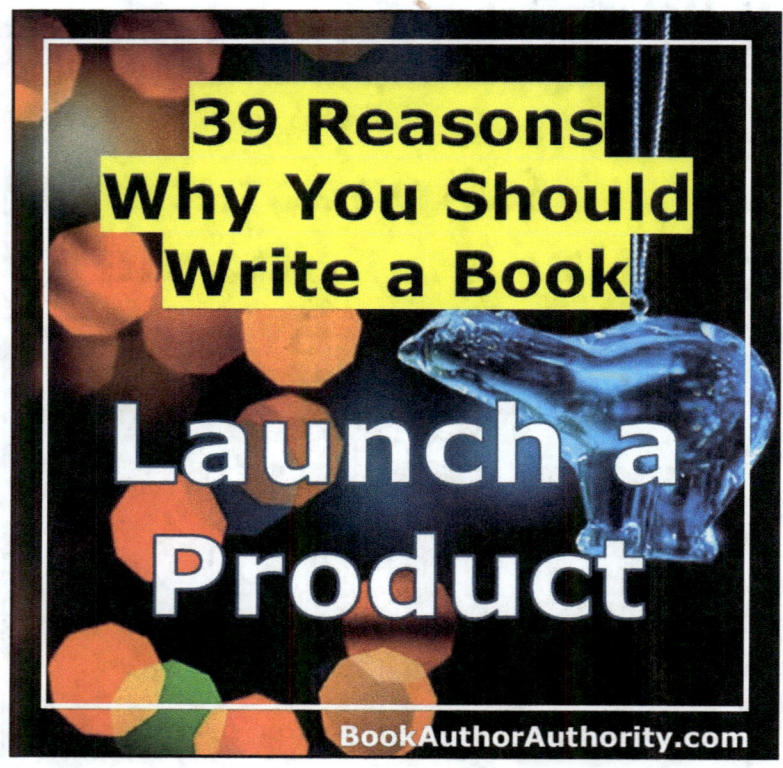

Use your book to anchor a high-ticket product launch, just as Mike Koenigs is using his book *Publish and Profit* as a giveaway to encourage people to explore the complete Publish and Profit program he launched at that time.

32. Become a product spokesperson.

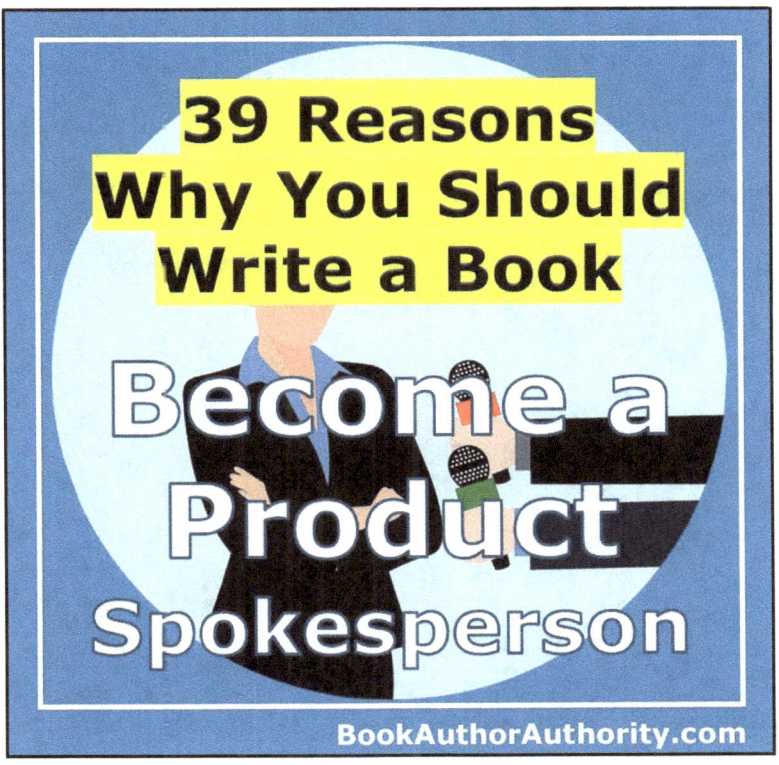

Companies and brands are always looking for people who can represent them well in their ads, their live consumer events, trade shows, conventions, and more. They are looking for YOU, the author of a book related to what their brand represents.

33. Sell rights.

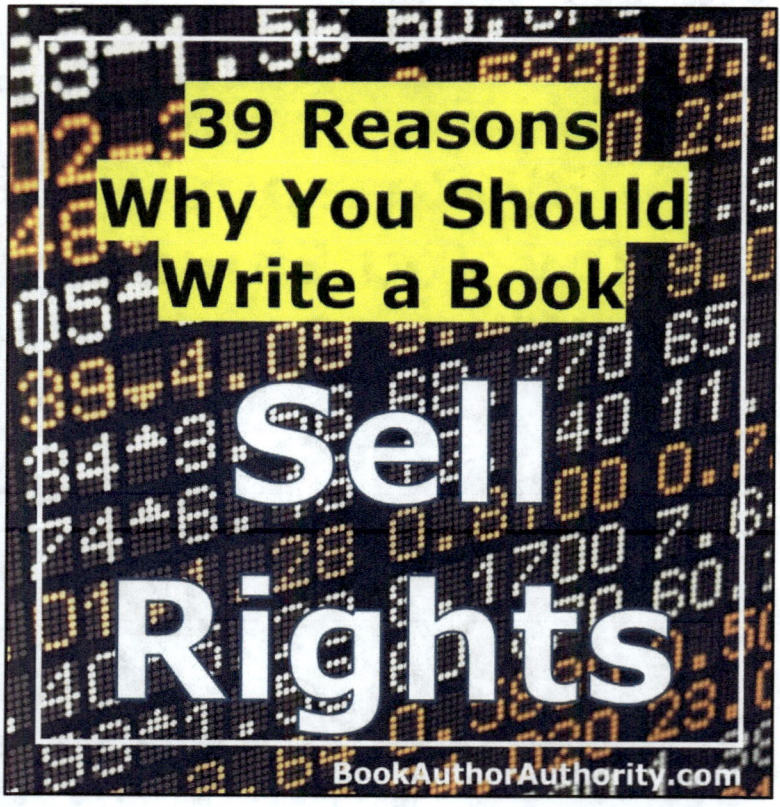

Every time you write a book, you create a constellation of rights around that book that can be sold: movie rights, reprint rights, foreign rights, audio rights, multimedia rights, merchandising rights, mass market paperback rights, online rights, and more.

J. K. Rowling did not become a billionaire from writing books. She became a billionaire by selling the ancillary rights those books automatically generated: foreign rights, mass market rights, movie rights, merchandising rights, and more.

34. Develop as a writer.

Someone who can write a book, can write almost anything: podcast episodes, blog posts, articles, columns, etc.

- ☐ As a book author, you immediately qualify to write for websites that pay money for blog posts and articles.
- ☐ As a book author, you could be invited to write a column for a related magazine.

☐ As a book author, you can also ghost write for other authors.

35. Help more people.

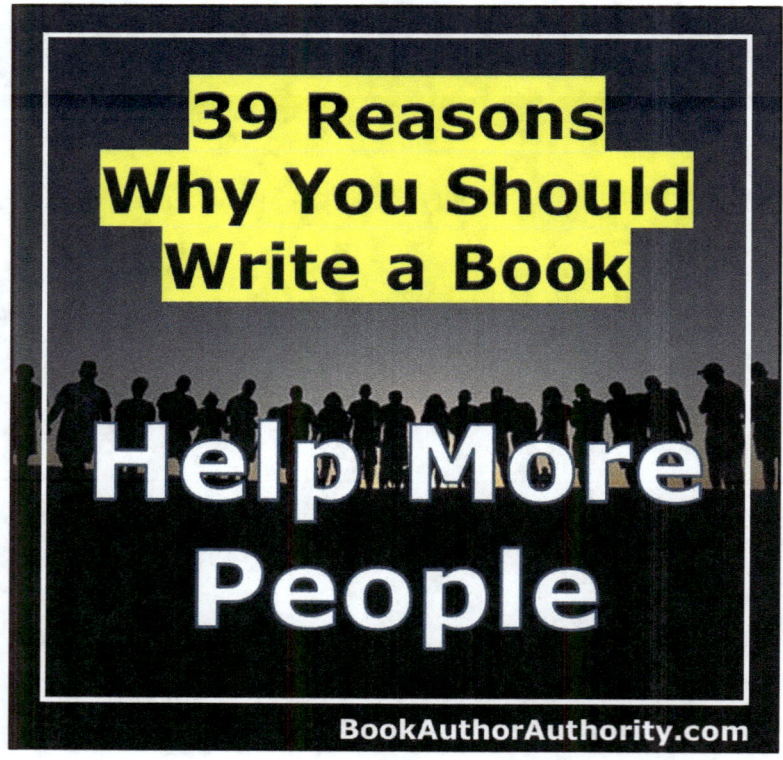

You can help a ton more people by writing a book that changes their lives than you can by donating your time at a food bank or by creating a new foundation.

36. Control your message.

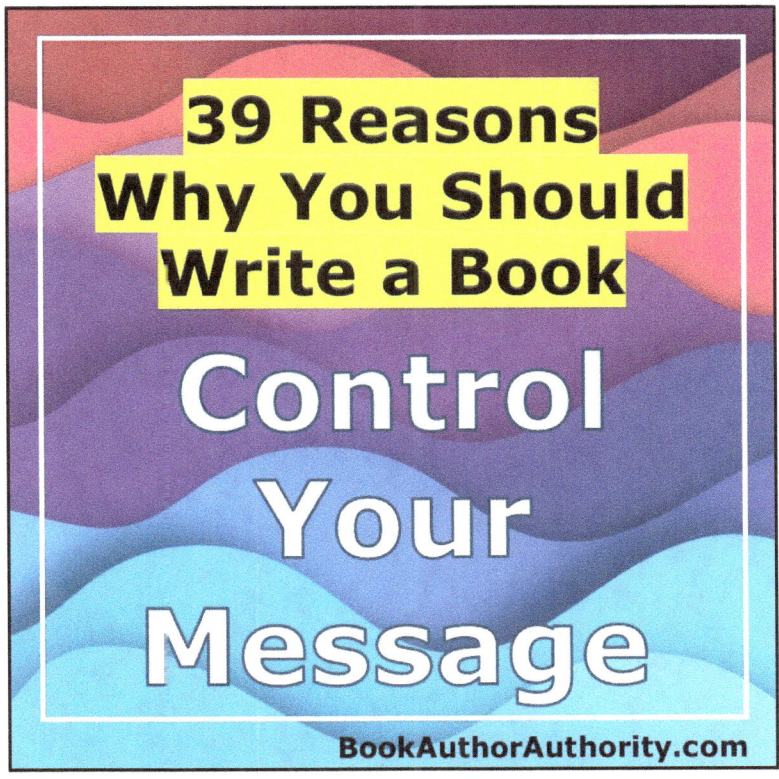

If you don't write your ideas down into a book, someone else might try to do it for you.

That is one reason Chip Wilson, founder of Lululemon, chose to write and self-publish his book, *Little Black Stretchy Pants*: "It's one of the reasons I wrote the book; if you leave the press to write the story, they won't get it right."

As he noted, "I know from reading about other companies that the press rarely gets more than 2% correct."

37. Promote other products.

When the founders of Away discovered that their first production run of suitcases was not going to be ready for the holiday season, they created a high-end travel book and sold it with a gift card for a free suitcase (to be redeemed in February when the production run would be completed).

38. Establish an institute.

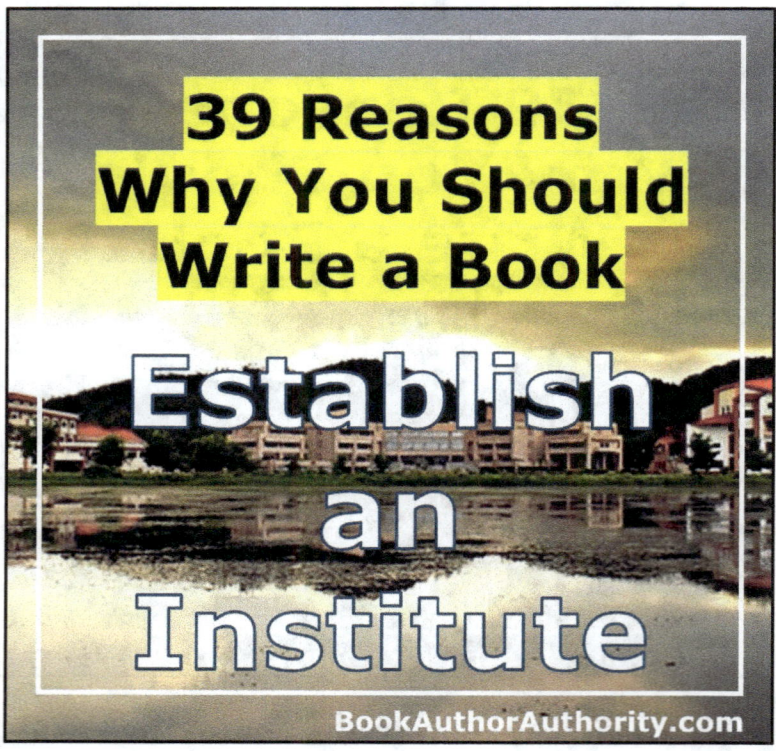

More than one author has created an institution to carry on their work originally inspired by the book they wrote.

Jeffrey Smith, author of *Seeds of Deception*, founded The Institute for Responsible Technology to provide health information to consumers about the risks of genetically modified food.

39. Found a movement.

Why stop at a book? Why stop at an institution? Why stop at a series of products? Why not create a movement? A movement that changes the world?

Are you ready to change the world? One book at a time. One story at a time. One person at a time. Mind to mind. Heart to heart. Soul to soul. Spirit to spirit. Universe to universe.

18 Points on Why You Should Write Children's Books!

Check out these 18 reasons why you should write children's books (besides loving the child inside yourself):

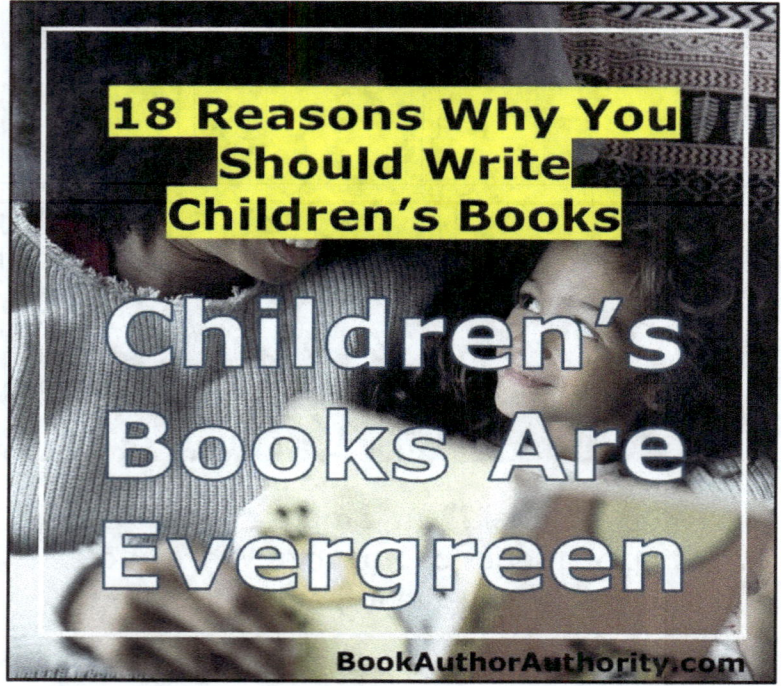

1. Children's books are evergreen. They never go out of style.

2. Children's books are in great demand. Sales grew 475% in one year alone.

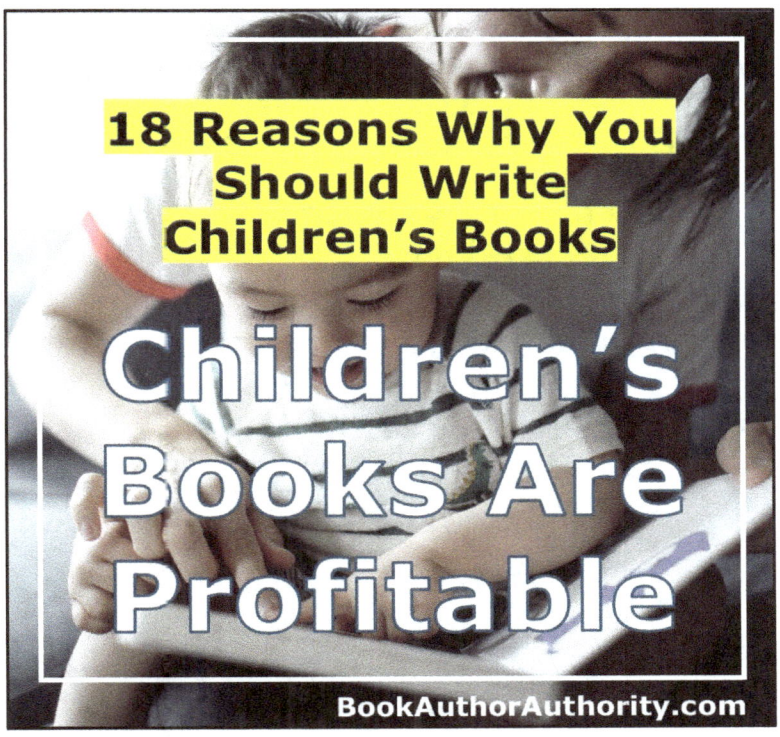

18 Reasons Why You Should Write Children's Books

Children's Books Are Profitable

BookAuthorAuthority.com

3. Children's books are profitable. They can provide thousands of dollars in royalties every month.

4. Children's books are easy to promote online because there are tons of blogs, podcasts, and YouTube channels devoted to books, children, and mommy bloggers.

5. Parents are happy to spend money on them. Children's books are like virtual babysitters.

6. Grandparents also love to buy books for their grandchildren!

7. Children's books are fun to write!
Writing is as simple as telling a story to your children, your nieces and nephews, or your grandchildren—or your neighbor's children!

8. Children's books can be written in a few hours. They generally are less than a few thousand words.

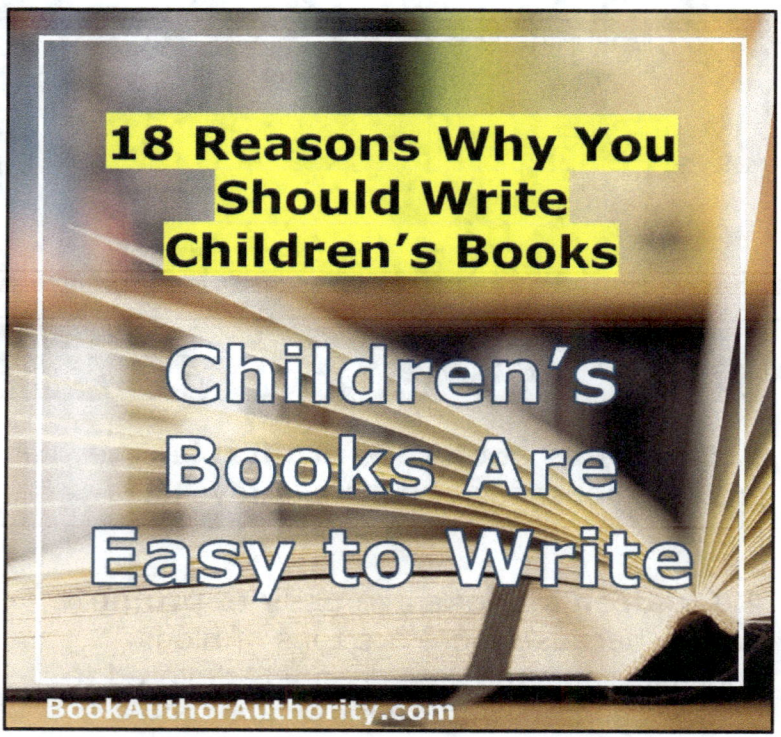

9. Children's books are easy to write, once you create a system.

10. Children's books are easy to outsource if you don't want to create them yourself—but then you'd miss all the fun!

11. Children's books are largely image-based. That means you have less words to write, but it also means you need an illustrator if you want to publish the books yourself. Or use a great A.I. program to create the images for you.

12. Children's books can be formulaic. Once you hit on a formula, you can rinse and repeat.

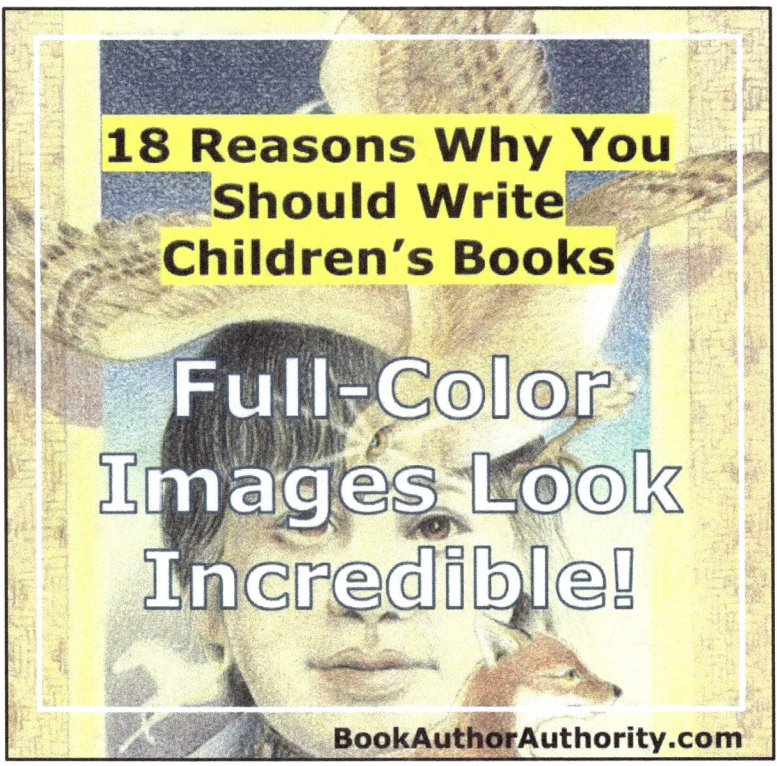

13. The full-color images in children's books look great in Kindle Fire, on the iPad, or in other ereaders (or even in a colorful PDF).

14. Children's book covers are easy to create. Use an image from the book, the book title, and a template (especially for series).

15. It's easy to create a bestseller, with so many categories and subcategories available for kids.

16. Children's books are easy to merchandise what with their emphasis on images and brandable characters. You can add images from the book to t-shirts, mugs, umbrellas, and more. Or license the images to a great merchandiser.

17. Children's books make great series:
Judy Blume, Goosebumps, Wimpy Kid,
Grossology, Nancy Drew, Eyewitness Books,
Ballpark Mysteries, The Boxcar Children,
Madeline, etc.

Once you've created a number of children's
books in a series, you can compile them and
sell them as an omnibus collection.

**18. Children's books make great audio
books** that children can listen to again and
again. The cost to record an audio reading of a
children's books is a lot less than what it costs
to record a 600-page novel or 200-page
nonfiction book.

18 Reasons to Write Books for Children

- ❑ **Children's books are evergreen.** They never go out of style.
- ❑ **Children's books are in great demand.** Sales grew 475% in one year alone.
- ❑ **Children's books are profitable.** They provide thousands of dollars in royalties every month.
- ❑ **Children's books are easy to promote online.** There are tons of blogs devoted to books, children, and mommy bloggers.
- ❑ **Parents happily spend money on them.** Children's books are like virtual babysitters.
- ❑ **Grandparents also love to buy books for their grandchildren!**
- ❑ **Children's books are fun to write!**
- ❑ **Children's books can be written in a few hours.** They are less than a thousand words.
- ❑ **Children's books are easy to write**, once you create a system.
- ❑ **Children's books are easy to outsource** if you don't want to create them yourself — but then you'd miss all the fun!
- ❑ **Children's books are largely image-based.** That means you have less words to write.
- ❑ **Children's books can be formulaic.** Once you hit on a formula, you can rinse and repeat.
- ❑ **The full-color images in children's books look great in Kindle Fire and iBooks!**
- ❑ **Children's book covers are easy to create.** Use an image and a template.
- ❑ **It's easy to create a bestseller**, with so many categories and subcategories available for kids.
- ❑ **Children's books are easy to merchandise.** Put images on a t-shirt or license for other products.
- ❑ **Children's books make great series:** Judy Blume, Goosebumps, Wimpy Kid, Grossology, Nancy Drew, Boxcar Children, Madeline, etc.
- ❑ **Compile several books** and sell them in an omnibus collection.

10-Point Checklist: What Do You Want to Get from Your Book?

Before you write your book, you should decide what you want to get out of your book being published?

Circle the up arrows of any of the following results that you would like to accomplish with your new book:

Become a *New York Times* bestselling author.

Get paid $1,000 per hour for your coaching and consulting.

Appear on major national TV shows or podcasts as an expert (*The Today Show, The View, Gutfeld,* etc.).

Get paid $10,000 to $60,000 when you speak.

Have customers willing to pay $500, $2,000, $10,000, or more for a product you create.

Change lives with your book.

Have newspaper and magazine editors knocking on your door to interview you.

Drive tons of traffic to your website, podcast, social media, etc.

Become a social media superstar and tribal leader with tens of thousands of fans.

Become a social media superstar and tribal leader with tens of thousands of fans

BookAuthorAuthority.com

Have websites, bloggers, and podcasters clamoring to feature you.

The above ten points are just a few of the results that can happen when you create and promote a bestselling book. Even a slow selling book can product incredible results!

Once you know what you want, you can create an even better book. Go for it!

Once you know what you want, you can create an even better book!

BookAuthorAuthority.com

About John Kremer

John Kremer is the author of *1001 Ways to Market Your Books*, mentor to authors who have sold over a billion books, and founder of the Billion Book Initiative to help the next generation of book authors sell another billion books.

Over the past 40 years, he has helped thousands of authors, both major celebrities and those just starting out, to sell more books! Lots more books!

John is 75 years old. His wife Gail, a storyteller, is author of *Little Fox and the Golden Hawk*. They live in a small town in Arizona, where they take care of a dog named Poe.

Would you like to become an authority on your topic— and do it within ten days from today?

Become an Authority on Any Topic

Would you like to become an authority on a topic of your choice? What do you have to do to become an authority? Simple: You write a book on that topic.

If you are having trouble getting around to writing a book, or you are simply having trouble finishing what you have written, or things sometimes seem to get too complicated, read on ...

Would you like to become an authority on your topic, any topic—and do it within ten days from today?

Then hire me to write a book for you, and I will deliver an incredible and powerful authority-building book to you within 10 days.

I'll write a book for you that is an 80- to 120-page book to establish you as an authority for the key words or concept or topic you want to own. No matter the topic.

I'll write a book that will establish you as an authority on food, travel, business, entertainment, spirituality, music, movies, online marketing, love and romance, success, self-help, art, writing, design, project management, gardening, poetry, biography, fiction, or any of a hundred other topics. Your choice of topic.

My job is simple: To write you a book that will establish you as an authority, not an expert but an authority, on any subject.

The book I write will not be created by AI. No writing by AI. No content from AI. No graphics from AI. AI does not increase your authority or credibility.

AI sucks!

If I don't think that I can write a book on your topic, I'll tell you. Straight up. No bull. And I'll tell you before you send any money. I'll be very clear.

For this quick and powerful service, my fee is $3,000 upfront. But, here's my guarantee: If you don't like the book I write for you, I'll refund your payment. No questions asked.

If you don't like it, I'll publish the book under my name and become an authority on one more subject (I'm already an authority in a dozen fields).

You can upload the book to Amazon, Ingram Spark, Bublish, Lulu, Smashwords, BookBaby, or Blurb for sale, but the main purpose of the book is to establish you as an authority and to use the book as a giveaway to build your email list of potential customers.

Here Is What You Get

An 80- to 120-page book targeted to your key words, concept, or topic. This book will establish you as an authority on your subject! Value: $10,000 on up!

Ready to Sell — A book written, edited, designed, and formatted, ready to be uploaded to Amazon and/or Ingram Spark or other ebook and book publishing sites. Value: $500 or more!

A Selling Book Cover — A book cover designed to sell your book and build your authority. Value $3,000 or more.

A Giveaway PDF of the book designed to be used as a bonus to build your email list. Value: $1200 or more.

80 to 100 branded images ready for sharing on your favorite social media networks, including Facebook, Instagram, LinkedIn, Pinterest, Truth Social, xTwitter, and others. Value: $30 per image or $2,400 to $3000!

A Powerpoint template that will allow you to create 10 or more YouTube videos from those images. I'll show you how easy it is to create these videos! Value: $400 or more.

Total value: more than $18,000!

Start today. Don't wait. Do it now!

Ready to get started? Let's talk! Just email me at BookPromotionExpert@gmail.com or call me at 575-741-1581.

Let's get started today!

John Kremer
575-741-1581